STEP 4
WORKBOOK

The questions in this workbook are my own version of similar questions that are used by members of various 12 step fellowships. I will be forever grateful for the knowledge and wisdom that is passed on by those who went before us.

A free printable PDF version of the questions, for use by individuals in their own recovery, is available on my website at https://jobimia.wixsite.com/podencopress/step4workbook

WHO IS THE WORKBOOK FOR?

Before you read further, I want to give you the opportunity to decide if this Workbook is the right choice for you.

If you are happy to write out a full life story and believe you can do that without missing out important aspects, you probably don't need this Workbook.

If you can remember all the fears, sexual misdeeds and resentments that have impacted your life, without the need for assistance, this Workbook is not for you.

But if you are concerned that you will not be able to complete a thorough inventory without questions and prompts to trigger memories, and additional areas to record patterns and names of people who deserve an amend, this Workbook is for you.

INTRODUCTION

During my time in recovery I have met many thousands of people. Most have walked through the doors of their respective recovery rooms desperate, but even as their life has improved and they have begun to work the Steps, almost everyone has doubted their ability to surrender sufficiently to undertake Step 4. Some people I know have even hesitated in getting a sponsor and beginning the Steps, just so they could avoid Step 4 altogether.

This workbook is, in a way, my attempt at finding a solution to my own Step 4 difficulties. I have seen similar sets of questions in various fellowships but none, I believe, provide quite this structure.

The funny thing is, it is never really Step 4 they are afraid of, even though to work it requires the opening of emotional arteries to release the pain of the past. Just as we used our addictions to avoid our emotions, so these people refused to do their fourth step to avoid the inevitable - sharing their secrets with a sponsor in Step 5.

First, I want to reassure you that Step 5 is a release, not a hurdle. When I left my sponsor's home, having shared my Step 5 with her, a rainbow appeared in front of my car and remained with me constantly as I drove to my home. To say I felt the weight being lifted by working Step 4 would undoubtedly be an understatement.

So, assuming you have decided to tackle this Step, you must decide which of the many ways you wish to work it. Many write it out the AA Big Book way, with columns detailing their fears, resentments and sexual misdeeds. This way has the advantage of helping you identify what character defects caused you to feel and behave the way you did, and also to identify people to whom you owed amends.

I tried Step 4 that way but my mind went blank. However hard I tried, sitting in front of a table of columns wracking my brain to recall my resentments, was not sufficient that by the end I felt I had produced a fearless and thorough inventory.

Others write a life story and work with a sponsor to identify patterns of behavior, and people they had harmed, from that. Again, I think my attempt at a life story turned out to be a few scrawled pages of disorganized stream of consciousness.

HOW TO USE THE WORKBOOK

On the following pages you will find questions and writing prompts split into three sections: your childhood, adolescence and adulthood. Each section aims to draw out the most important aspects from that period of your life, as well as delving into your fears, resentments and sexual misconduct.

At the end of each section are pages for both character defects and amends lists. These pages aim to give you a head start on first Steps 6 & 7 (character defects) and second Steps 8 & 9 (amends list). Here is how I suggest you use the different pages in this workbook.

QUESTIONS AND PROMPTS

Simply answer all the questions in each of the childhoold, adolescence and adulthood sections as fully and honestly as you are able.

CHARACTER DEFECT LIST

Read through your answers to the questions in the relevant section with an eye to spotting patterns of character defects as you read. Then list all the defects you find on the pages allotted to this task. You can do this yourself as you work the Step or you may prefer to enlist your sponsor's help during your Step 5/6.

AMENDS (PEOPLE HARMED) LIST

Read through your answers to the questions in the section you are completing, and write down all the names of people who have been affected by your behaviour. You might end up with a long list, but that doesn't necessarily mean each and every person will be due an amend.

Remember, you are making amends to people you have harmed. Your sponsor will be able to help you decide which amends are necessary when you work Step 8 together.

GRATITUDE LIST

At the back of this workbook I have added space for you to begin writing a gratitude list. I recommend adding at least 5 items to a gratitude list every day.

Being grateful helps us build emotional resilience, ready to draw on during challenging times in your recovery.

JOURNAL PAGES

This section can be used for countless different purposes. Here are some great examples of what you can do with it:

- Write affirmations.
- Journal about your day.
- Journal your feelings.
- Step 10 daily review;
- List recovery actions taken.

EXAMPLES OF CHARACTER DEFECTS

- Resentment
- Anger
- Fear
- Cowardice
- Self-justification
- Self-centredness
- Guilt
- Dishonesty
- Impatience
- Greed

- Gluttony
- Arrogance
- Ungrateful
- Vengeful
- Thoughtless
- Irresponsible
- Self-hatred
- Low self esteem
- Prejudice
- Lust

- Jealousy
- Gossip
- Fantasizing
- Grandiosity
- Manipulative
- Self-importance
- Controlling
- Selfishness
- Procrastination
- Criticism

- Pride
- Ego
- Denial
- Envy
- Laziness
- Insincerity
- Negativity
- Perfectionism
- Judgement
- Intolerance

STEP 4
QUESTIONS
AND PROMPTS

Made a searching and fearless
moral inventory of ourselves.

CHILDHOOD

How did you feel on your first day of school? Did you find it easy to make friends?

If you were afraid of the dark, how did your parents respond? How did this affect you?

Did you steal things as a child? If so, what did you steal and why?

Did you get caught? If so, how were you punished?

Did you move homes as a child? If so, how often? Did you have to change schools or make new friends? Discuss how this affected you.

_____

_____

_____

_____

_____

_____

_____

_____

_____

_____

_____

_____

_____

_____

_____

_____

_____

_____

_____

_____

Were you richer or poorer than those around you as a child? Were you treated differently because of this? How did this affect you?

What was your health like as a child? Were you hospitalized? How did this affect you?

If you were separated from family as a child, how did you feel about it and how did it affect your development? Did you feel it was your fault? Did you feel guilt, shame, fear or anxiety? Do you feel that the separation caused harm to you?

If your parents lived separately, what was their relationship like?
How did this affect you?

What beliefs did your family have when it came to money? Were there conflicting values?

_____

_____

_____

_____

_____

_____

_____

_____

_____

_____

_____

_____

_____

_____

_____

_____

_____

_____

How did you react to your family members fighting?

How did your father get along with his parents?

Did your parents fight much? When they did fight, did you feel unsafe or afraid? Did you get drawn into their fights or feel you needed to stop them? Did they want you to take sides or did you do that naturally?

Were your parents religious? If so, did their religious beliefs affect you?

Did you observe or were you involved in other sexual experiences while still a child? If so, what were they and how did you they affect you?

Were you a planned baby? Did both your parents want you? Write about your family's situation when you were born. Include as much detail about your family situation as you can remember

Who raised you? If it was someone other than a parent, how did you feel about that? How do you think it affected you?

_____

_____

_____

_____

_____

_____

_____

_____

_____

_____

_____

_____

_____

_____

_____

_____

_____

_____

_____

_____

What were you afraid of as a child? Write down as many things as you can think of.

Did any family members or people other than your immediate nuclear family live with you when you were a child? How did this affect you?

Were you made to feel guilty or wrong when it came to early expression of your sexuality, or for your sexual orientation?

What role did you play within your family? What did your family think of you?

_____

_____

_____

_____

_____

_____

_____

_____

_____

_____

_____

_____

_____

_____

_____

_____

_____

_____

_____

_____

Write about your early sexual experiences, how your family behave around sex and your sexual development? How did you react to these experiences?

_____

_____

_____

_____

_____

_____

_____

_____

_____

_____

_____

_____

_____

_____

_____

_____

_____

_____

_____

How did you feel about introducing others to your family? Were you proud or ashamed of them? If so, why?

What was the overall atmosphere in your home when you were a child? Was there laughter and love, or anger, arguing and depression? How did this affect you?

Did either of your parents die when you were young? If so, in what way do you feel this affected you?

If you misbehaved, were you threatened? How did your fears affect you?

Did people say you looked or behaved like a family member? If so, what were they like and how did being compared to them affect you?

Did you ever see or hear your parents having sex? If so, how did you feel at the time and how did it affect you?

Were you affected by your ethnic or racial background? Were you different from your peers in any way? If so, did they treat you differently or were you discriminated against? How did it affect you?

_____

_____

_____

_____

_____

_____

_____

_____

_____

_____

_____

_____

_____

_____

_____

_____

_____

_____

_____

_____

How did your family's views and behaviors around money affect you?

_____

_____

_____

_____

_____

_____

_____

_____

_____

_____

_____

_____

_____

_____

_____

_____

_____

_____

Do you have older or younger brothers and sisters? How did you feel about them and how did they feel about you?

Did you have any awareness of your parents' sexual relationship? If so, how did it make you feel?

Were you expected to help around the house? Did you have chores and if so, were they fair or were you overburdened? How did this affect you?

How did your mother get along with her parents?

How were you punished/disciplined as a child? How did these punishments affect you?

Was there a time at school that things changed and your feelings changed about school? If so, what happened and how did it affect you?

If your parents were married, what kind of marriage did they have?
How did this affect you?

Did you fight with other children or your parents when you were a child? How did your family react to this?

Were either your parents or siblings hospitalized when you were a child? How did this affect you?

ADDITIONAL QUESTIONS FROM SPONSOR

ADDITIONAL QUESTIONS FROM SPONSOR

ADDITIONAL QUESTIONS FROM SPONSOR

ADDITIONAL QUESTIONS FROM SPONSOR

ADDITIONAL QUESTIONS FROM SPONSOR

CHARACTER DEFECTS LIST

PEOPLE HARMED LIST

ADOLESCENCE

What kind of friend were you to others?

Were you academic or sporty at school? Were you in a clique or an outsider? How did your experience at school affect you?

Did anything happen to you at school which affected you negatively? Did you drop out of school? If so, why?

_____

_____

_____

_____

_____

_____

_____

_____

_____

_____

_____

_____

_____

_____

_____

_____

_____

_____

_____

_____

Did you get in trouble during your adolescence? Did you steal, talk back, cause trouble, vandalize property? If so, why? Discuss.

Were you rebellious, resenting authority or popular kids? Did you have low self-esteem or were you egotistical? How did you get along with people at school in general?

How did your family members feel about sex and sexuality? How did their attitude, beliefs (including religious) and actions affect you and the development of your sexuality?

How did your friends and peer group's views on sex and sexuality affect you?

When did you first notice your sexual desires and orientation? How did you feel about them and how did you first act on them?

Did your sexuality impact in a negative way on your relationships with your peer group?

_____

_____

_____

_____

_____

_____

_____

_____

_____

_____

_____

_____

_____

_____

_____

_____

_____

_____

In adolescence, were you ever called names, (e.g. frigid, slut, homo etc) in regard to your sexuality or sexual prowess or identity? If so, why and how did it affect you?

Did you have friends, a best friend or a group of friends? How did your friendships impact your adolescence?

_____

_____

_____

_____

_____

_____

_____

_____

_____

_____

_____

_____

_____

_____

_____

_____

_____

Were you compared to your siblings or other family members?
How did this affect you?

Write about your first boyfriend or girlfriend. How were you affected by that relationship?

Did you get into fights or avoid conflict? Were you a bully or mean to less popular kids?

Were you a late bloomer or an early developer? Were you bigger or smaller than your peers? How did you feel about how you looked and your physical attributes?

Were you an outgoing child or were you shy? Did that change as you grew older? Do you judge shyness or brashness? Do you prefer large groups or being alone? If so, why?

How did you feel about your parents during your teenage years?
Why?

What were your feelings towards your siblings or other family members? Why?

What type of adolescent were you? Did you have moods and tantrums? How did you get along with the rest of your family at this time?

_____

_____

_____

_____

_____

_____

_____

_____

_____

_____

_____

_____

_____

_____

_____

_____

_____

_____

Were you caught lying? If so, how were you punished? How did you feel when you got caught?

_____

_____

_____

_____

_____

_____

_____

_____

_____

_____

_____

_____

_____

_____

_____

_____

_____

_____

_____

Write about some of the most embarrassing things that happened to you in your teens?

What was your most embarrassing sexual experience in your teens.
How did it affect you?

_____

_____

_____

_____

_____

_____

_____

_____

_____

_____

_____

_____

_____

_____

_____

_____

_____

_____

_____

What kind of teenager were you? Would you want to have been your parent? Why?

Write about your feelings about any other sexual experiences or masturbation fantasies during your adolescence

Were there any pregnancies or pregnancy scares in your adolescence? What happened? How did you feel about your actions?

Did you shop-lift or steal things? Why?

Were you a good or bad friend? Did you have one or more friends throughout your adolescence or did you break up with friends often or if someone 'better' came along? Why?

Did you fit in? Wear the same clothes and like the same things as your peers?

Did your parents have enough money to buy you the things you needed? If not, how did you feel about that?

_____

_____

_____

_____

_____

_____

_____

_____

_____

_____

_____

_____

_____

_____

_____

_____

_____

_____

_____

Did your sibling(s) get more than you did? Was there a favorite?
How did you feel about that?

Did you have to work for your allowance/pocket money? Did you have to work outside the home to get the things you needed?

Did you skip a grade or were you held back in school? Did you get good or bad grades? How did you feel about that?

_____

_____

_____

_____

_____

_____

_____

_____

_____

_____

_____

_____

_____

_____

_____

_____

_____

What were the best and worst things that happened to you in your teens? Why?

ADDITIONAL QUESTIONS FROM SPONSOR

ADDITIONAL QUESTIONS FROM SPONSOR

ADDITIONAL QUESTIONS FROM SPONSOR

ADDITIONAL QUESTIONS FROM SPONSOR

ADDITIONAL QUESTIONS FROM SPONSOR

CHARACTER DEFECTS LIST

PEOPLE HARMED LIST

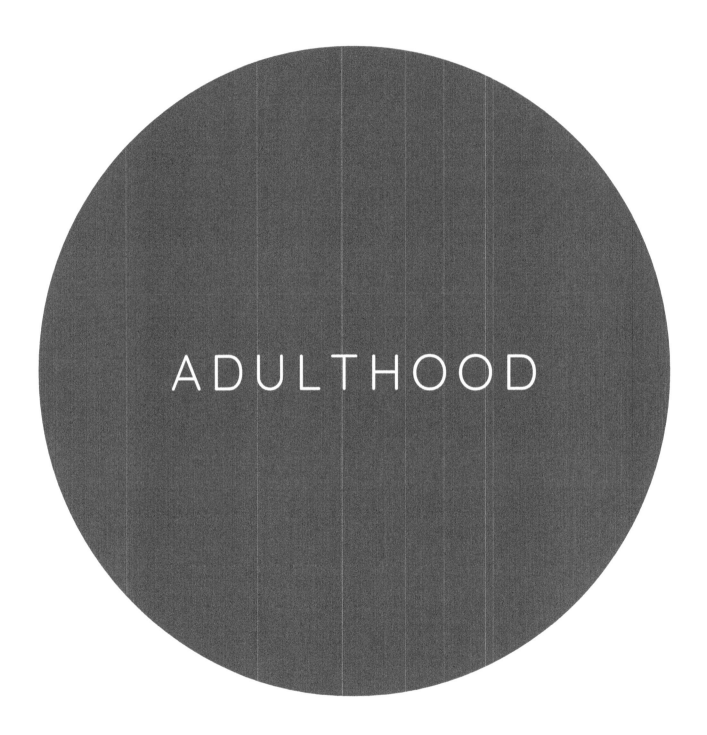

ADULTHOOD

Do you worry about the future? What sorts of things do you worry about?

Do you neglect the needs of your friends and family or your own needs? How?

Do you feel you are worthy of love or do you feel that you have to earn it?

Are you generally right? Do you become angry when people disagree with you or don't do what you say?

Are you emotionally available to your friends and family? If not, give examples where you have been unavailable and why.

Were you lonely and use sex to cover your loneliness? Did you accept sex in place of love? What was the result?

Did you marry someone who had similar traits to one or both of
your own parents? How were they similar? How did this impact on
your relationship?

_____

_____

_____

_____

_____

_____

_____

_____

_____

_____

_____

_____

_____

_____

_____

_____

_____

If you are married or in a long-term relationship (or have ever been), write about what is good and bad about your relationship? Why did you get married? Did you marry too young? Do you want to stay married? Discuss.

If you have never married (or been in a long-term relationship), why do you think this is? Would you like to be able to have this type of relationship? Discuss.

_____

_____

_____

_____

_____

_____

_____

_____

_____

_____

_____

_____

_____

_____

_____

_____

_____

_____

_____

Write down everything you remember stealing – include property and money but also consider other things such as time, attention, ideas, goodwill, relationships etc.

Have you felt ashamed of anything you have written in these questions? How do you feel your addiction / codependency impacted on your past behavior?

Do you manipulate or use people and situations to get what you want? How?

Do you gossip and put people down to feel better about yourself?
How?

Do you feel resentment toward your spouse/partner? Write what you are resentful about and why.

How do your spouse/partner get along with your family? Are you forced to take sides?

Do you still feel like the child in your family? Do you use this to your advantage? How do your family still take care of you?

Do you allow your spouse/partner to take care of you? Do you take advantage of their love? How?

Do people have to bail you out of trouble? How? How does this affect you?

Are you financially responsible? Write down the ways you have been financially irresponsible.

In what ways do you feel entitled?

Write down five instances when you have gossiped recently. How does gossip make you feel? How do you feel when others gossip about you?

_____

_____

_____

_____

_____

_____

_____

_____

_____

_____

_____

_____

_____

_____

_____

_____

_____

_____

_____

In what ways do you feel rules or laws do not apply to you? Do you feel your own situation is different from that of others? Why?

Write down all the resentments you still holdl today. Do you want revenge or for something bad to happen to the subject of your resentments? Why?

_____

_____

_____

_____

_____

_____

_____

_____

_____

_____

_____

_____

_____

_____

_____

_____

_____

_____

_____

Write down how you feel the following areas of your life are going at the present time: relationship / recovery / friendships / work / sex / family / finances / spiritual.

Do you spend an appropriate amount of time on each area of your life? How could you achieve more balance in your life?

_____

_____

_____

_____

_____

_____

_____

_____

_____

_____

_____

_____

_____

_____

_____

_____

_____

_____

_____

Write about any sexual experiences you have not yet mention which cause you embarrassment or guilt that you have not discussed

Do you use sex as a reward or punishment or to boost your ego?

Do you feel awkward or have fears around sex? Discuss.

How do you feel about how you look? Do you have shame around your physical appearance? In what ways

Having answered these questions, how do you feel about your pre-recovery life?

Do you fear rejection? How does this affect your behavior and relationships?

Have there been times you have rejected others or put barriers between yourself and others, to avoid being rejected? Give examples.

Write down what love means to you.

Do you consider yourself a responsible person? In what ways do you not act responsibly?

Are you financially responsible? Are you a miser or do you spend when you should not?

Have you been dishonest with money and expenses? Give examples?

Do you feign illness? Or do you use it as a reason for your behavior or to get what you want? How?

Do you resent anyone at work? If so, why?

Are you jealous of anyone, either at work or elsewhere? Do you harbor negative feelings towards your boss or your work mates? What kind of employee are you?

Are you paid well? Could you do your boss's job better than he or she can?

How do you feel about your partner? Write about your relationship. What do you feel guilty, resentful or fearful about in your personal relationship and with your children?

How do you feel about your children (if you have any)? Do you use your children against your spouse, do you ask your children to choose between you?

_____

_____

_____

_____

_____

_____

_____

_____

_____

_____

_____

_____

_____

_____

_____

_____

_____

_____

_____

Do you have unreasonable expectations of your partner or children?

Do you think your life would be better / easier without your partner or children? In what ways?

Do you feel people take you for granted? How?

Do you feel superior or inferior to others? How does this affect your serenity and recovery?

_____

_____

_____

_____

_____

_____

_____

_____

_____

_____

_____

_____

_____

_____

_____

_____

_____

_____

In what ways do you judge other people?

In what ways do you compare yourself to others? Do you come up lacking or do you feel superior? Give examples.

How did your selfish sex conduct harm yourself or others? List all instances you can remember? Who was hurt and how?

How did your selfish sex conduct affect your personal relationships, your work, and other relationships?

How did you react to these situations? Did you feel guilty or justify
your behavior?

How did your sexual frustration affect others? Did you take your frustrations out on people? Did you withdraw from the relationship or become angry? Discuss.

_____

_____

_____

_____

_____

_____

_____

_____

_____

_____

_____

_____

_____

_____

_____

_____

_____

_____

_____

Were you promiscuous? Did you blame others for your behavior?

_____

_____

_____

_____

_____

_____

_____

_____

_____

_____

_____

_____

_____

_____

_____

_____

_____

_____

Do you take time to care for your appearance? If not, Why?

Are you vain? Do you judge yourself and other people by appearance? Why?

Are you envious, prideful or boastful? Are you defensive and vengeful when someone points out your mistakes? Give examples.

Write a list of resentments you still hold

What lies do you tell and why?

Write down examples of when you have been grandiose. How do you feel when you are bragging to someone?

Do you feel superior because of your background, finances or education?

Do you respect others time, and treat them with respect and kindness?

Are you happy? Do you resent people who seem to be happy when you are not? Do you know what it means to judge other people's outsides to your inside

Are you angry at life? List the things you are angry about.

What are your greatest fears today?

What one thing / event are you most afraid of? Why?

Write down any goals or wishes you have for your recovery.

_____

_____

_____

_____

_____

_____

_____

_____

_____

_____

_____

_____

_____

_____

_____

_____

_____

_____

ADDITIONAL QUESTIONS FROM SPONSOR

ADDITIONAL QUESTIONS FROM SPONSOR

ADDITIONAL QUESTIONS FROM SPONSOR

ADDITIONAL QUESTIONS FROM SPONSOR

ADDITIONAL QUESTIONS FROM SPONSOR

CHARACTER DEFECTS LIST

PEOPLE HARMED LIST

GRATITUDE
LIST

Gratitude List:

Gratitude List continued:

Gratitude List continued:

Gratitude List continued:

JOURNAL

Made in the USA
Monee, IL
25 August 2020